WELCOME TO URQUHART CASTLE

Today, the setting of Urquhart Castle is tranquil, with superb views across Loch Ness and the rugged landscape beyond. But this is no mere picturesque ruin. The beauty of the scene conceals centuries of turmoil and bloodshed.

The site has good natural defences, and a Pictish fort probably once stood here. The stone castle was built around 1230 by the Durward family, installed by Alexander II to assert royal authority in the Highlands.

The castle itself enters the historical record in 1296, when it was captured by the invading army of Edward I of England. From the mid-1300s it was a Scottish royal castle, but further strife came in the 1400s and 1500s as Islesmen from the west swept up the Great Glen, initially to assert power and later to plunder. The final siege was during the Jacobite Rising of 1689–90. When the government troops left in 1692, they blew up the gatehouse, leaving the castle impossible to defend.

Visitors can now enjoy a peaceful ruin with a long and eventful history.

CONTENTS

Top left: The Grant Tower, the most prominent structure on the site, under a brooding sky.

Opposite: The gatehouse, with its twin towers, was built around 1300 as the castle's main entrance.

HIGHLIGHTS

▶ **THE EXHIBITION**
Before visiting the castle itself, it is well worth exploring the exhibition, which includes some of the extraordinary artefacts found at the site, a scale model of the castle, information about the medieval household and a short film charting the history of the site.

▼ **THE GATEHOUSE**
An imposing and well-defended twin-towered entrance dating from around 1300. As well as controlling access to the castle, it provided accommodation for the constable and for any prisoners in his charge (p.12).

◀ **THE GRANT TOWER**
The most recent surviving building on the site, a five-storey tower house built for the Grant family, probably in the mid-1500s (p.22).

▲ **VIEWS OF LOCH NESS**
Climb to the summit for the best view up and down the Great Glen and the vast loch – the second-largest in Scotland – which for many centuries formed the main route to and from Glenurquhart and the castle (p.8).

▲ **THE TREBUCHET**
A modern replica of a medieval siege engine, one of the most feared weapons of the Middle Ages. Edward I's army may have used military technology like this when besieging the castle. (p.33).

This page: Urquhart Castle in winter, seen from the north-east.

URQUHART CASTLE AT A GLANCE

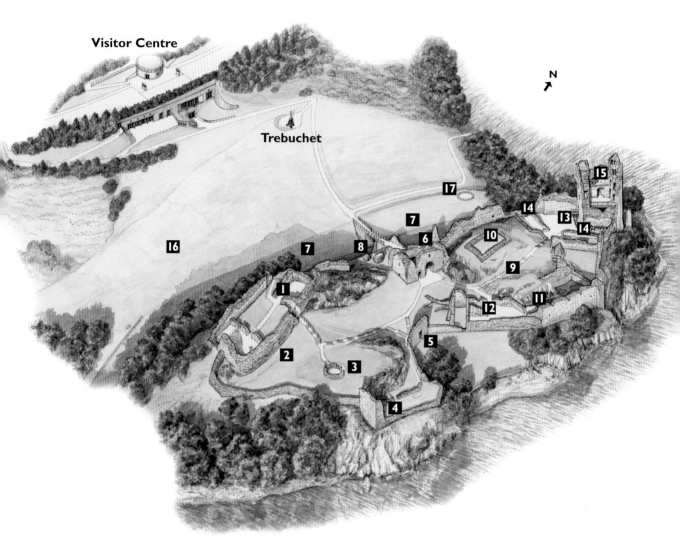

Visitor Centre

Trebuchet

N

1 SUMMIT
Site of the earliest evidence of fortification, probably from at least Pictish times. This area continued in use as the main focus of the castle until the late 1200s.

2 UPPER BAILEY (SERVICE CLOSE)
When the focus of settlement shifted to the northern half of the site in the 1300s, this area probably housed stables and workshops.

3 DOOCOT
The wall footings of a beehive-shaped building of the 1500s where pigeons were housed as a source of meat for the castle's residents.

4 SMITHY
The south gable and low west wall of a building on the edge of the loch. It seems to have been used in various ways, perhaps latterly as a smithy.

5 WATER GATE
Providing access to the loch at a time when waterways provided the most efficient form of travel.

6 GATEHOUSE
A well-defended entrance to the castle added as part of a major development in the late 1200s or early 1300s. Deliberately blown up by departing government troops after the first Jacobite Rising of 1689–90.

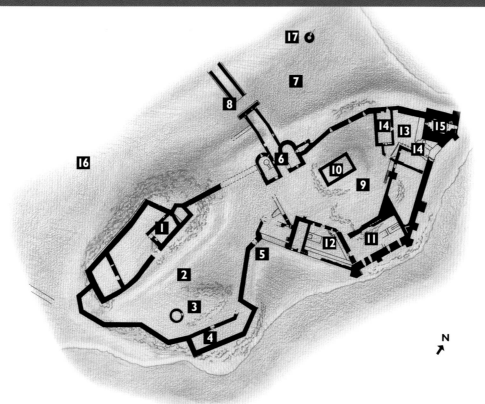

7 DITCH

Cut from solid rock to help defend the castle's vulnerable landward side, possibly in the early 1200s.

8 SITE OF DRAWBRIDGE

The drawbridge allowed access to the castle but could be bolted closed in case of attack. A high-walled causeway connecting it to the castle provided strong defensive positions and a facility for counter-attack.

9 NETHER BAILEY

A courtyard providing access to the great hall, chapel and associated buildings from around 1300, when the focus of the castle shifted to the north.

10 CHAPEL

Only the wall footings survive of a small rectangular building that may well have served as the castle's chapel.

11 GREAT HALL CELLARS

The great hall was the main public room of the castle from about 1300 until about 1500. Only the cellar level, used for storage, now survives.

12 GREAT KITCHENS

Added in the 1300s, probably as a kitchen serving the adjoining great hall. The water inlet survives, along with a mass of stonework, probably a base for the central hearth above.

13 INNER CLOSE

A courtyard associated with the Grant Tower, containing the service buildings required by the Grant household.

14 KITCHEN

Either of these two buildings may have served as the kitchen for the Grant Tower.

15 GRANT TOWER (SITE OF DONJON)

Probably built around the middle of the 1500s, this fashionable five-storey tower house was the main residence in the final century of the castle's life.

16 SITE OF CASTLETOUN

The area to the west of the castle would once have been filled with life and noise, as the craftsmen serving the castle's residents went about their business.

17 KILN

A furnace of unknown purpose, associated with later occupation of the site.

A GUIDED TOUR
OF URQUHART CASTLE

This tour follows a broadly chronological route around the castle ruins, beginning at the highest part of the upper bailey and ending at the opposite end of the castle, at the tower house constructed by the Grant lairds.

The castle sprawls across two mounds on an hourglass-shaped promontory, surrounded on three sides by water. The setting provides good natural defences – though it is overlooked by higher ground on the western landward side.

This site first appears in the historical record in the 500s AD, and continued in use until 1692. Its denuded rubble walls bear witness to a violent history, particularly from the late 1200s onwards.

Much of the dressed stonework and architectural detailing has been removed or destroyed. As a result, our ability to interpret the remains of this once magnificent medieval stronghold has been irreparably compromised. Important archaeological discoveries, together with insightful reading of the architectural and documentary evidence, have filled in many of the gaps in our knowledge, but much remains open to interpretation. We encourage you to draw your own conclusions.

The tour begins at the summit, the highest part of the castle, to your right as you leave the visitor centre. To get there, follow the path down across the bridge and through the gatehouse. On your way you will pass the trebuchet, a replica medieval siege engine, which you can read about on page 33.

Left: The castle seen from the visitor centre, with Loch Ness beyond. Across Loch Ness lie the Erchite Woods. The 'military road' running along the loch's far shore was originally built by General Wade following the Jacobite Risings of the 1700s.

THE EARLIEST CASTLE

The highest part of the promontory was probably the earliest to be occupied. It is well defended, providing a clear view of the landscape surrounding Urquhart Castle, and across Loch Ness in particular.

Some traces of early occupation have been found here. Vitrified (fused) stone was discovered in the 1920s, which may indicate the presence of a fort. Indications of intense heating, which causes rocks to melt and bond, are sometimes found on fortified sites dating from about 500 BC until AD 500. The vitrified stone, combined with radiocarbon dating from timbers excavated in the 1980s, suggests that the site may have been occupied as early as the 500s AD.

The earliest surviving stonework dates to the 13th century and is associated with the acquisition of Urquhart by Alan Durward. Durward built a 'shell keep', a stout stone structure encircling the top of a hill. This may have incorporated a small stone tower at one end. The walls protected the more vulnerable timber buildings within.

A ditch was dug to strengthen the defences, and a timber palisade may have been erected to enclose the rest of the area defined by the ditch. Coull Castle in Deeside, another Durward fortification, developed along similar lines. Built in 1228 and destroyed in 1307 by Robert Bruce, it illustrates how Urquhart might once have looked.

The palisade was replaced with a stone wall in the late 1200s, by which time the focus of occupation had shifted to the northern half of the enclosure. The shell keep at the summit was reoccupied in the 1400s. This may be a reflection of Urquhart's role in the conflict between the Crown and the MacDonald Lords of the Isles over possession of the earldom of Ross. Glen Urquhart was attacked repeatedly in the 1400s, which must have prompted the desire for an elevated stronghold.

Top left: The remains of the fortifications at the summit, site of the first stone castle, where traces of earlier defences have also been found.

Left: The site of Coull Castle, principal seat of the Durwards.

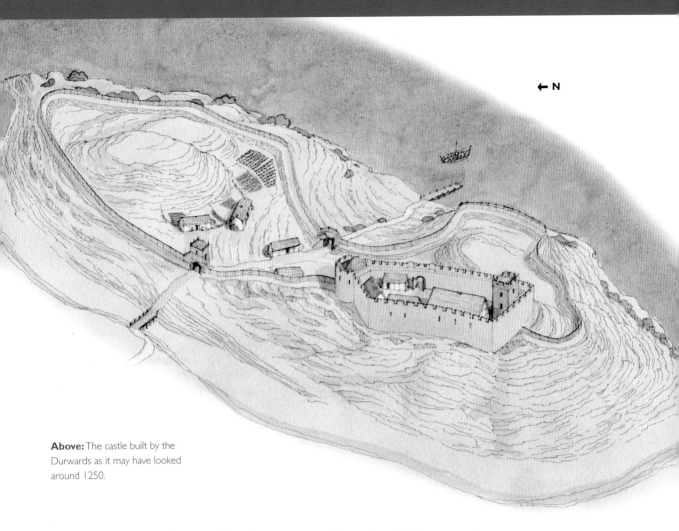

← N

Above: The castle built by the Durwards as it may have looked around 1250.

Many artefacts from the 1400s have been recovered from the shell keep, mostly from the southern summit. The concentration of material may suggest that the buildings on the shell keep were abandoned in a hurry during one of the many turbulent episodes in the castle's late-medieval history.

Archaeological finds from Urquhart paint an unusually rich picture of life in the medieval castle. The high proportion of deer bones indicates the importance of hunting for the nobility. Gaming pieces and fragments of musical instruments point to familiar leisure pursuits. Pottery imported from the Low Countries is a reminder that the castle was linked into trading networks, exporting timber and furs via Inverness.

Depart via the stairs and descend towards the circular structure in the grass.

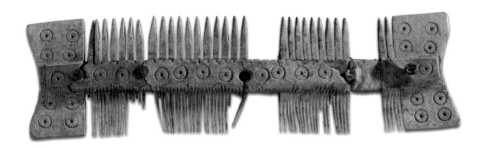

Left: A comb of carved antler found at the site and now displayed in the visitor centre. The ring and dot pattern was popular in medieval times.

THE UPPER BAILEY (SERVICE CLOSE)

The area of the castle below the summit is known as the upper bailey. When the focus of settlement shifted to the northern half of the enclosure in the late 1200s or early 1300s, this area may have become a service close.

The buildings which facilitated everyday life in the castle were probably sited here. These would have included the brewery, bakery and stables, probably largely built from timber. This part of the castle continued to serve the practical requirements of Urquhart's occupants into the 1500s.

The south gable of a large building built in the 1300s stands on the lochside below the shell keep. It has been suggested that this was a guesthouse and latterly a smithy. Few features survive from which to draw conclusions, but it is likely the building had several uses over its lifetime. Like many of the buildings at Urquhart, it probably made good use of the ample supplies of timber available locally in its construction. Timber slots survive in the west wall.

Top left: The stables as they may have looked in medieval times. We cannot be sure where they were located, but the building that once stood near the water gate is a likely candidate.

Left: The footings of the circular doocot.

Above: Iron horseshoes and a nail of a kind used to fix them in place. They probably date from the 1300s or 1400s.

The one recognisable structure is the circular doocot on the terrace below the summit. This doocot is typical of Scottish doocots built in the 1500s, and is almost certainly the 'dove-grove' referred to in a charter of 1509. Four nesting-boxes survive. Doocots were common features in medieval castles, providing a regular supply of pigeon meat and eggs.

At the narrow waist of the hourglass-shaped promontory, and almost directly opposite the gatehouse, is the water gate. This gate gave access to the loch shore and was an important means of entry and exit in medieval times. In an age when roads were easily rendered impassable, most of the provisions for the castle would have come by boat and been offloaded below the water gate.

The loch was also an important food source. Although river fish were eaten at Urquhart, cod was more popular. This was perhaps because the sea provided a reliable supply that could be brought in by boat, whereas catches from the loch could fluctuate. To the north of the water gate are the footings of a small building attached to the kitchen, which opens onto the loch. This may have been used for net storage or boat repairs.

Between this store and the water gate is the footprint of another building. This would have been a convenient location for a stable. Guests might have dismounted here on entering the courtyard through the gatehouse.

Return towards the gatehouse through which you entered the castle.

Below: The water gate, which allowed goods and people to access the castle from the loch.

THE GATEHOUSE

At the end of the 1200s the castle was held by the powerful Comyn lordship. They almost certainly constructed the stone curtain wall around the promontory, with this formidable gatehouse as its main entrance.

Above: The gatehouse as it may have looked when in use. The portcullis was operated from a chamber above the entrance passage. The porter's lodge lay on the ground floor, on the north (near) side. He and the constable probably slept in chambers on the upper floors.

The structure is similar to the contemporary gatehouses at Kildrummy and Bothwell, but also to those at Welsh castles such as Harlech, demonstrating the close architectural links between England and Scotland in the 1200s. Harlech was commissioned by the English king Edward I, and Kildrummy's gatehouse may have been his work too.

The gatehouse served two functions. It controlled entry into the castle and provided residential accommodation, probably for the constable. In the absence of the lord, the constable was responsible for the daily running, maintenance and defence of the castle. From the gatehouse he could control admission to the site.

At ground level is the entrance passage, wide enough to allow carts to pass through. It was strongly defended. A portcullis – a grating of bars – protected the outer portal, raised and lowered from an upper floor. Its grooves can still be seen. Further into the passage were two additional barriers. These were either stout timber doors or open-barred iron grilles called yetts. The passage between the portcullis and these inner doors was covered by a timber deck containing 'murder holes', through which defenders could shoot or hurl objects at attackers.

On the north side of the passage a door leads to the guard room or porter's lodge. The porter was responsible for checking visitors' credentials during the day and ensuring the castle was securely locked and barred at night. He rang a bell at the top of the gatehouse to signify the 'hours' dividing up the household's day and signalled the change in the night watch. He also guarded any prisoners in the prison cell, which can be seen within his lodge.

There is a second gatehouse lodge in the south tower, entered from the courtyard. This was later converted into a kiln-house, where corn was dried and stored.

The first floor of the gatehouse, now reached by a modern spiral stair, comprises a two-roomed lodging – a hall and chamber. This was probably the constable's accommodation when his lord was in residence. From here, he could control access into the castle. Above the porter's lodge is a hall – a reception room; above the kiln-house is his chamber, a retiring room where he slept, in the large bed recess. Both rooms had fireplaces and latrines.

The space directly over the entrance passage originally gave access to a room high above the outer portal. This chamber housed the winding mechanism for the portcullis.

In 1689 came the first in a string of Jacobite Risings which aimed to restore the Stuart monarchy to the throne. At this time the castle was garrisoned by troops loyal to the reigning monarchs William and Mary. On their departure in 1692, they ensured that the Jacobites could not make use of the castle by destroying the gatehouse with gunpowder. Some remains from those upper rooms lie on the grass to the west of the gatehouse; they incorporate chimney flues.

Above right: The twin-towered gatehouse, deliberately blown up by the departing government forces in 1690.

THE DITCH AND THE CASTLETOUN

From the top of the gatehouse you can get a good view of the great ditch which defends the landward side of the promontory.

This ditch was allegedly created by Alan Durward in the early 1200s, although it has never been accurately dated. Hacked out of solid rock, it divided the rocky knoll on which the castle sits from the broad open terrace to the west, similar to Durward's castle at Coull, Deeside.

The ditch was constructed to protect the landward side of the castle, which was most vulnerable to attack. It was connected to the castle by a stone causeway, part of which survives. A fixed bridge now replaces the drawbridge which once spanned the gap.

The medieval drawbridge would have been a heavy and robust timber structure. It was operated from the castle side of the ditch using a timber superstructure that has long since disappeared. Large vertical sockets for its uprights survive in the stone foundations on the castle side of the ditch. There are also stone buttresses on both sides of the ditch. These were designed to counteract the immense thrust of the timbers and the lifting mechanism.

The causeway between the drawbridge and gatehouse was enclosed within stone walls. Now reduced to footings, these walls were once fitted with arrow-slits and housed two gates, or sallyports, via which the garrison could exit to engage the enemy while the drawbridge remained locked and barred.

Beyond the ditch was the castletoun, a noisy, industrious settlement filled with tanners, woodworkers, metalworkers and more. The remains of Urquhart's castletoun were found when archaeologists investigated the site of the visitor centre before it was constructed.

Leave the gatehouse and turn left towards the tower house.

Above: The ditch, probably dug in the early 1200s to defend the castle from the landward side. It was spanned by a drawbridge, now replaced by a modern wooden bridge.

THE NETHER BAILEY

The northern half of the promontory, known as the nether bailey, was the heart of the castle from the late 1200s onwards.

Its earliest known occupation is contemporary with the construction of the curtain walls. In addition to the curtain walls and gatehouse, a donjon – a fortified residential tower – was built where the later Grant Tower now stands. The great hall, later joined by a kitchen and chamber, faced out over the loch. On a knoll in the centre of the nether bailey was a small rectangular building. It has been suggested that this was the castle's chapel.

With the exception of the gatehouse, the buildings of the late 1200s and early 1300s have been reduced to foundations and low walls. We cannot be sure when they fell from use, but most if not all had probably been abandoned by 1509, when the Grants received permission to rebuild on the site. As early as 1527, Hector Boece referred to the 'rewinous wallis' of Urquhart Castle.

By the 1700s, the castle seems to have looked much as it does today. As a result, it is hard to identify how the structures were originally used, although other medieval castles can provide useful analogies.

There are several reasons to believe that the buildings represented in the ruins of the nether bailey were not all in use at the same time. Urquhart had been subject to repeated attacks in the 1300s and 1400s, which would have caused substantial damage. We know from the 1509 grant of Urquhart to John Grant of Freuchie that rebuilding was necessary, but we cannot be sure whether the whole site required reconstruction. This seems unlikely, based on the evidence of the buildings that are attributable to the Grants – and what is known of castle building elsewhere in the 1500s.

Below: The nether bailey as it may have looked in the early 1300s, when the focus of the castle had shifted to the north. The donjon, or residential tower, stands at the far north (left), on the site now occupied by the Grant Tower.

← N

At some point in the early to mid–1500s,
the Grant Tower was built on the site of the
medieval donjon. This new building, and its
associated ranges, are fortified in a way very
different from the great defended courtyard
castles of the 1200s and 1300s. Easier to defend,
more private and more comfortable, the Grant
Tower reflected the different requirements
of the new lairds and the changing role of
Urquhart Castle in the aftermath of the
conflicts of the 1400s.

Top: The nether bailey, with the gatehouse to the left.
The ruined building on the mound at the centre is
thought to have been the chapel.

Right: The chapel as it may have looked when in use.

THE GREAT HALL RANGE

Facing onto the loch is a crescent-shaped row of rectangular structures, the earliest of which is the great hall at the centre of the range.

The hall was the main living space and had many functions. It was used for the administration of the estate and for feasting; it was also where the household staff ate, socialised and slept. The lord and his family would have had private chambers. The great hall was probably built in the late 1200s or early 1300s for the Comyn family, who may also have been responsible for the gatehouse. It was raised over a basement which contains what may be a masonry support for the base of a central hearth in the timber-floored hall above. During the 1300s a kitchen was added to the south end of the hall and a great chamber to the north.

The great chamber was a private space to which the lord could retire. A similar room was provided in many castles of this period. The chamber was accessed from the north end of the great hall. It had thinner walls than the hall and, like most of Urquhart's buildings, made good use of timber in its construction. The surviving basement walls have slots which once held the timbers supporting the floor above.

Above: The great hall as it may have looked when the Comyns were in residence, around 1300. Only the cellars of the buildings in this range now survive.

The fragmentary great kitchens retain their water inlet. A central doorway, flanked by two windows, leads into the basement from the courtyard. Food would have been carried upstairs, probably into a servery adjoining the hall. There is a small extension at the west end of the kitchen which has no obvious function. It opens into the loch, and has no openings onto the courtyard or into the adjacent building. It is therefore likely that its function related to the loch.

At some point in its history, the hall was rebuilt with thinner walls and divided by a wall along its length. This suggests a major change of use and may be related to a period of unrest in the late 1300s and 1400s. The chamber seems to have fallen from use around this time, as a latrine from the remodelled hall emptied into its basement.

Right: A view along the lochside from the Grant Tower. The cellars of the great hall range are visible at the far left of this photograph.

THE URQUHART EWER

'Remember the day we found the teapot?'
John McDonald of Glen Urquhart,
Ministry of Works workman 1921.

The 'teapot' was found by workmen clearing the castle ruins in 1921. It is in fact a very fine example of a ewer, or water jug, probably made in the 1400s. The bronze ewer once had a hinged lid, now lost. Such an object would have been used for washing hands over a flat bottomed bowl, in which the ewer would stand when not in use.

This page: The ruined service buildings added around the inner close by the Grant lairds are now dominated by the Grant Tower.

THE GRANT BUILDINGS

It is possible that the older and probably ruinous buildings in the nether bailey were demolished by the Grants during their occupation of the site in the 1500s, although we can't be certain of this.

If the older buildings were indeed damaged and without a use, they may have been considered unsafe and so deliberately taken down or buried. The principal area of occupation was now centred on the remains of the medieval donjon tower. A new tower house was built here using the ruins of the donjon, and a small cobbled courtyard was formed around it. The basement of the old tower was buried to create a level surface. This was walled off from the nether bailey and entry into the new close was barred by a gate. The original stone gutter still drains the close, but the enclosing wall has been reduced to footings.

Two other buildings were accessed from the close. The building to the west of the Grant Tower has fireplaces at both ends, indicating that it was divided in two. This may be the kitchen referred to in the 1509 charter. However, neither fireplace is as large as might be expected for such a purpose.

Little can be said about the building to the south of the Grant Tower, except that its undercroft was probably a storeroom. It was built on the footings of an earlier latrine tower and part of the great chamber. A fragment of walling between this building and the tower may be part of a bread oven, suggesting that the Grants' kitchen was in fact located here.

Below: An illustration from a cookery book published in Germany around 1500 gives an impression of a kitchen of the period.

THE GRANT TOWER

The most prominent feature of Urquhart Castle is the tower house at the northern end of the promontory. This was built by the Grant family in the 1500s.

In December 1509 James IV gave Urquhart Castle to John Grant of Freuchie. At the time, however, the castle was probably in poor condition and certainly not a fit residence for a prominent lord. The charter stipulated that Grant should:

'repair or build at the Castle a tower, with an outwork of stone and lime, for protecting the lands and the people from the inroads of thieves and malefactors.'

The resulting tower is five storeys high, and the entrance leads into the second of these, the hall. The hall was the least restricted of the rooms in the tower, an outer reception room that may also have been put to limited use for dining. It was lit by good-sized windows and heated by a large fireplace in the south wall. A narrow spiral stair leads down to a dimly-lit stone-vaulted storeroom in the basement and a well-defended postern, or back entry. The thick basement walls were probably part of the medieval donjon.

A second spiral stair leads to the upper floors. It is likely that the parapets and turrets at the top were added towards the end of the 1500s, or even in the early 1600s. The refinement may even have been the handiwork of James Moray, master-mason, who was carrying out major repairs at the castle as late as 1623. Much of the tower's south wall has collapsed, probably during a 'storme of wind' in February 1715. Nonetheless, the building retains much of its sense of space and grandeur as a residence of nobility.

We do not know exactly how the upper floors were used, but we can speculate. The fine room directly over the hall was most likely the Grants' outer chamber, a more private space where the lord and lady could relax and entertain close friends. They would have dined here when not entertaining in the great hall. Above that was their inner chamber, also a reception room, but reserved for their most intimate companions. It would also have contained an elaborate bed.

The top storey had a garret in the main tower, perhaps for the use of minor members of the family. Square-gabled turrets at the corners each contain a little chamber, complete with a fireplace, a window and a magnificent view of the glen.

Top left: The Grant Tower, the most complete building in the castle. Its south wall collapsed during a storm in 1715, but all floors are still accessible.

This page: One of the gunholes in the Grant Tower.

THE HISTORY OF URQUHART CASTLE

This page: A painting of 1878 by the English artist John Everett Millais (see page 47).

The rocky promontory on which Urquhart Castle stands juts out into Loch Ness, amid one of the most dramatic and beautiful settings in Scotland. The loch forms part of the Great Glen, a long valley filled with lochs and rivers, leading from the Atlantic to the North Sea. For centuries, water was the main means of transport in the region.

Despite its fame, Urquhart Castle has not received as much attention from archaeologists and historians as might be expected. It is difficult to reconcile the castle's dramatic story with the surviving rubble stonework, but the ruins are a product of its historical and physical prominence. From its appearance in the historical record in Pictish times to its abandonment in 1692, there is no doubting Urquhart's importance in the history of northern Scotland.

AIRCHARTDAN

The first written reference to Urquhart appears in St Adomnán's *Life of St Columba*, written in the late 600s. The name means 'by the wood or thicket'.

Around AD 580, St Columba travelled through the Great Glen on a long and arduous journey to the court of Bridei, king of the Picts, at Inverness. Adomnán tells us that he baptisted Emchath, a dying man who had 'preserved his natural goodness all through his life', at a place called Airchartdan or Urquhart. Not only Emchath but his whole household, from his son Virolec down, were baptised. When the ceremony was complete, Emchath 'gladly and confidently departed to the Lord'.

It is not certain that Emchath's residence was on the promontory where Urquhart Castle now stands. However, the discovery here of a fragment of Pictish brooch has led to speculation that his residence was in much the same position. Archaeologists have discovered evidence that this was a well-fortified place around Columba's time (see page 8). It was certainly an ideal site for a fort, surrounded on three sides by the deep waters of the loch, easily defended from the landward side and commanding extensive views.

Other missionaries followed in the footsteps of Columba. Christianity was mapped over the existing landscape of sacred features. In the hills just north of Drumnadrochit sits the square barrow cemetery of Garbeg (from the Gaelic car bheag, 'the little circle'). A Pictish symbol stone found here dates to around the same time as an incised cross from Temple, whose name is an anglicised form of *an teampull*, meaning 'chapel'.

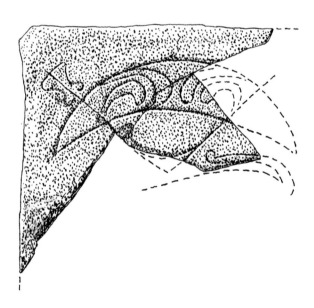

Above left: Columba baptising the dying Pict known as Emchath. According to a biography of Columba, this episode took place at Airchartan on the Great Glen, tentatively identified as Urquhart.

Above: An illustration of a Pictish carved stone found at Garbeg Farm, near Urquhart.

Left: A fragment of a Pictish silver brooch found near the castle.

COLUMBA AND THE WATER BEAST

Today, many people visit Urquhart Castle not only to view the ruins of a once-mighty medieval castle, but to try to catch a glimpse of the famous 'Loch Ness Monster'.

Tales of mythical water-beasts have long been associated with Highland lochs. But the sighting of a monster in or around Loch Ness was first recorded in Adomnán's biography of Columba, written around AD 700. The unforgettable moment is described as follows:

'When the blessed man stayed for some days in the land of the Picts, he had to cross the River Ness. When he reached its bank, he saw some of the local people burying a poor fellow. They said they had seen a water beast snatch him and maul him savagely as he was swimming not long before … The blessed man, having been told all this, astonished them by sending one of his companions to swim across the river and sail back to him in a dinghy that was on the further bank …

'Luigne moccu Min obeyed without hesitation. He took off his clothes except for a tunic and dived into the water. But the beast was lying low on the riverbed, its appetite not so much sated as whetted for prey. It could sense that the water above was stirred by the swimmer, and suddenly swam up to the surface, rushing open-mouthed with a great roar towards the man … The blessed man looking on raised his holy hand and made the sign of the cross in the air, and invoking the name of God, he commanded the fierce beast, saying:

'"Go no further. Do not touch the man. Go back at once."

'At the sound of the saint's voice, the beast fled in terror so fast one might have thought it was pulled back with ropes … The brethren were amazed to see that the beast had gone and that their fellow-soldier Luigne returned to them untouched and safe in the dinghy, and they glorified God in the blessed man.'

Above: St Columba as depicted in stained glass at St Margaret's Chapel in Edinburgh Castle. He travelled widely from his base at Iona and probably visited the Great Glen.

TIMELINE

DURING THE 500s	AROUND 580

A FORT
is probably established on the summit.

ST COLUMBA
reputedly travels in the Great Glen, visiting a Pictish settlement near Inverness that may be on or near the site now occupied by the castle.

THE FIRST CASTLE?

Above: Sir Alan Durward depicted meeting local chiefs in his castle at Urquhart.

In 1230 Alexander II granted the lordship of Urquhart to the powerful Durwards, one of several noble families brought to the region to help maintain royal authority. The Durwards soon set about fortifying the promontory.

The Durwards were an Angus family whose name derives from the hereditary post of the king's door ward. Alan Durward, whose father's estates were centred around Coull and Lumphanan on Deeside, was given the estate of Urquhart around 1230.

It is possible that Urquhart was part of an existing estate before Durward took over, but there is no evidence to support the existence of an earlier fortification here. In the 1100s, numerous motte and bailey castles were being built in Moray, then a huge province embracing most of the Great Glen. This was a mark of the penetration of feudalism, a system by which the Crown could ensure that lands were governed by trusted men.

However, the clearest indication that kings of the 1100s were bringing Moray under control is provided by the establishment of churches, as each new estate required a church to receive tiends, or tithes. By the early 1200s Kilmore was already the parish church of Urquhart, perhaps indicating that the estate was already being managed on behalf of the Crown.

Durward's castle at Urquhart took advantage of natural topographic features, as did the contemporary castles at Dunstaffnage and Tioram. It consisted of a stone citadel and a bailey, protected by a palisade, which contained ancillary buildings.

From the 1100s, castles constructed along the length of the glen protected trading burghs such as Inverness. These foundations brought economic development and established trade routes, but their distinctness as imposed settlements was recognised by the local population. One difference was linguistic. Gaelic was spoken less in the burghs and castles than in the glens.

The issue had been vividly demonstrated in 1228, when the people of Moray rose up against Alexander II. The king moved ruthlessly to crush the rebellion, and by Christmas 1230 he was celebrating victory in Elgin, the province's chief town. But it was clear that royal control could not be taken for granted.

Below, left to right: Castle Tioram in Loch Moidart and Dunstaffnage Castle near Oban. Built around the same time as Durward's castle at Urquhart, they are both strategically sited on rocky outcrops.

1230

ALEXANDER II grants the lordship of Urquhart to Sir Thomas Durward.

AROUND 1231

SIR THOMAS DURWARD dies and is succeeded by his son, Sir Alan, who probably builds or completes the first stone castle at Urquhart.

THE ESTATE OF URQUHART

Urquhart Castle was the centre of a vast estate reaching from Loch Ness to the mountains far to its west.

We have no details of the extent of the estate granted to the Durwards in the 1230s. However, thanks to the survival of royal charters granted to Sir James Grant and his two sons in 1509, we have a remarkably accurate picture of the extent of the ancient lordship and the settlements within it at that date.

The estate was vast, roughly the size of the Isle of Man. It enveloped both Glen Urquhart and Glen Moriston to its south, and extended from the fertile cornlands beside Loch Ness, inland over good pasture as far as the rich hunting-grounds of the Cluny Forest high in the mountains to the west.

Below: The sprawling estate associated with the castle includes the fertile valley of Glen Urquhart. In medieval times, hunting would have been a popular pursuit in these forests.

The medieval castle was closely connected with the surrounding estate. The lord's own demesne, or domain, was located at Borlum on the higher ground overlooking the castle to the west – this land was retained to support him and his household. The name Borlum is derived from 'boardland', meaning 'land for the lord's table'.

The parish of Glen Urquhart and Glen Moriston probably corresponded with the estate boundary. The parish had a single church at Kilmore as its focus, but in a parish of this size other holy sites were also necessary in order to serve the dispersed population. These included St Ninian's at Temple, which housed a relic of St Drosten and served as the main church for people living in the vicinity.

Timothy Pont, the first person to map the area in the 1580s, wrote that: 'certain hieland men and woemen doeth travell to this chappell at a certane tyme of the yeare, expecting to recover there health againe and doeth drink of certaine spring and wells'.

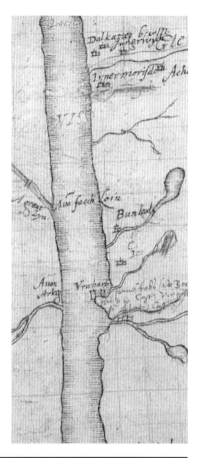

Above: Wild deer still roam the hills around Urquhart.

Above right: Urquhart as shown on Timothy Pont's map, the earliest attempt to chart this region.

DID YOU KNOW . . .

Bone gaming pieces known as 'tablesmen' have been found at Urquhart Castle. These were used in a popular game derived from the Roman game of *tabula*, the ancestor of backgammon. The gaming pieces from Urquhart have not been securely dated, but we know this game was popular from the 1200s onwards.

1249

A GRAND SHIP is built at Inverness for the French crusader Hugh, Compte de St Paul et Blois.

1275

JOHN COMYN, LORD OF BADENOCH AND LOCHABER receives the estate of Urquhart following the death without male heir of Alan Durward.

THE WARS OF INDEPENDENCE

Alan Durward died in 1275 without a male heir. His estate reverted to the Crown, and Alexander III granted it to John Comyn, Lord of Badenoch and Lochaber.

The Comyns were one of the most influential families in Scotland in the 1200s. They greatly embellished Urquhart Castle, turning it into a stone-built fortress with a high curtain wall, gatehouse, hall and tower.

However, their ownership of the castle was short-lived, due to major upheavals at the end of the century. In 1286, King Alexander III died, leaving his three-year-old granddaughter Margaret of Norway as heir.

Above: The siege of 1303, at which Edward I's forces recaptured Urquhart Castle.

She died in 1290, while on her way to Scotland for her inauguration. This power vacuum led to the 'Great Cause', a struggle between two rival claimants to the throne – John Balliol, Lord of Galloway and Robert Bruce, Lord of Annandale.

Edward I of England was invited to arbitrate. With his blessing, Balliol was inaugurated at Scone on St Andrew's Day 1292, and Scotland had a monarch for the first time in six years. The Comyns were Balliol's main supporters in the north, and it probably seemed as if local supremacy would continue unchallenged during his kingship.

But King John's reign was turbulent and brief. After he refused to render feudal service to Edward in his war in France, the English king responded by invading Scotland. The army that swept into Scotland in March 1296 met with little resistance, and Balliol was forced to abdicate. The great castles of Scotland were captured, Urquhart among them.

In the general rising against Edward of 1297, Sir Andrew Moray, a powerful local nobleman, attempted to retake Urquhart. He was unsuccessful, but did succeed in ousting the English from Moray.

In 1297, Sir William FitzWarine, constable of Urquhart Castle, wrote to Edward: 'On Monday morning Andrew de Moray and Alexander Pilchys with their abettors besieged the castle. In a night assault, William Puer and the writer's son were killed. The besiegers then drew off.'

Sir William seems to have escaped the glen shortly afterwards, and was later appointed as constable of Stirling Castle. Urquhart was back in Scottish hands by 1303, when English forces returned to lay siege. The constable, Sir Alexander Forbes, put up a spirited defence, sending his pregnant wife through the English lines before staging a counter-attack. This failed, however, and the castle was taken by the English. In 1304, the Comyns sought peace with Edward, who installed Sir Alexander Comyn of Badenoch as his new constable at Urquhart.

In 1306 Robert Bruce, grandson of Balliol's rival, murdered his own rival John Comyn, at the church of Greyfriars in Dumfries. We may never know whether Bruce planned this first strike against his great rival, but he claimed the throne soon afterwards. His battle against the Comyns gained momentum after the death of Edward I in 1307.

Bruce swept up the Great Glen, taking the Comyn strongholds as he went. A garrison was installed at Urquhart, and Thomas Randolph, his nephew and one of his most loyal supporters, was given the castle as a reward.

Right: Stone balls found on the site may well have been used as ammunition for a trebuchet.

THE TREBUCHET

The siege engine at Urquhart today is a working replica. It was built by an international team in 1998, and successfully deployed, hurling a boulder about 200 yards at a speed recorded as 126mph. No wonder, then, that trebuchets were greatly feared by those defending castles in the centuries before cannons appeared.

There is no written evidence that a trebuchet was ever fired during the many sieges of Urquhart Castle. However, we know that Edward I of England, whose forces besieged the castle in 1303, deployed similar devices during his military campaigns in Scotland. At Stirling Castle in 1304, he refused to allow the beleaguered garrison to surrender until he had shipped the dreaded War Wolf up the coast from south-east England and bombarded them with it.

Stone balls found at the site may well have been ammunition for a siege catapult.

Right: The replica trebuchet made at the site in 1998.

1297

SIR ANDREW MORAY besieges Urquhart Castle. He is unsuccessful, but ultimately drives out the English.

1307

KING ROBERT I (THE BRUCE) recaptures Urquhart Castle and uses it as a power base to bring the north-east under his control.

THE CASTLE AS RESIDENCE

Urquhart Castle was a major settlement which was not only a stronghold but also a civic centre, estate office, barracks, law court and prison.

In its 400-year history, the castle was never the main residence of the families who possessed it. The chief seat of the Durwards was at Coull, and the Grants, who held Urquhart in the twilight of its days, resided mainly at Freuchie (now Castle Grant) beside Grantown-on-Spey.

For most of the intervening years, Urquhart was a royal castle, though only one king of Scots ever slept here – David II in 1342. The castle would normally have been looked after by a constable, who was responsible for fortifying and maintaining it.

The constable played a particularly important role at Urquhart in the 1300s, and we know the names of many of those who resided here.

Above: The constable's lodging in the upper floor of the gatehouse, as it may have looked when in use. The little alcove to his left would have contained his bed.

For example, Sir Robert de Lauder held the castle against the English in 1334 and remained constable of the castle until 1359, when he was succeeded by his grandson.

Interestingly, there are no references to a steward at Urquhart. The steward was charged with maintaining the household and managing the estate, whereas the constable's role was more defensive. It is likely that at Urquhart the two roles were combined.

Medieval lords were constantly on the move, attending their king and sittings of parliament, visiting their peers and of course fighting wars at home and overseas. They also had to visit their estates to dispense justice and consume their rents, most of which were paid in kind (corn and animals) rather than cash. Urquhart had access to one of the best hunting reserves in Scotland, the royal forest of Cluny, which the lord of Urquhart administered on his sovereign's behalf. The importance of hunting at Urquhart has been backed up by the discovery of deer bones during excavations at the site.

Wherever the lord went he was accompanied by his retinue. When its master was in residence, the castle was crowded, warm and noisy. At other times it would have been largely empty. Not only did the household follow the lord around, so too did most of his furniture and furnishings. Evidence from elsewhere in Scotland suggests that the lord of Urquhart may have kept a household of well over 100 people.

During David II's visit in the summer of 1342, not only the sovereign and his travelling household were in residence but also two bishops, Moray and Ross, and three lords: Sir Robert de Lauder (the constable), Sir John de Kerdale and Sir William de Moubray with all their attendants.

Above: King David II of Scotland (left), who stayed at Urquhart in 1342. In this medieval manuscript, he is shown shaking hands with King Edward III of England at the end of the long Wars of Independence.

Above, clockwise from top left: A bronze brooch found at the site, dating from the 1300s or 1400s; a ceramic fragment found at the site, moulded to form a comical face; a modern reconstruction of the knight's jug of which it was once a part, decorated in a style popular in the 1300s; an iron spur found at the site, dating from the 1400s.

AROUND 1312

THOMAS RANDOLPH, EARL OF MORAY
receives the castle and barony of Urquhart as one of a number of honours from his uncle, Robert I.

1342

DAVID II
visits the castle during the summer, becoming the only monarch ever to sleep within its walls.

ROYAL URQUHART AND THE LORDS OF THE ISLES

After the Wars of Independence,
Urquhart was a royal castle, held for
the Crown by a succession of constables.

In 1371 the crown passed to Robert II. Robert granted
Urquhart to David, Earl of Strathearn, his fourth son.
By 1384 it was in the hands of his elder brother,
Alexander Stewart, Earl of Buchan.

Unpredictability and a volatile temper were
known qualities of the so-called 'Wolf of Badenoch',
and David soon had cause to complain about his brother's
mismanagement of the estate. However, the Wolf appears
to have been on good terms with his constables, and the
1300s saw Urquhart reach the peak of its development.
A chamber and kitchens were added, creating a range
of buildings along the lochside. Despite this expansion,
the nobles who held the castle were largely absent.

Lawlessness remained a problem in the estate,
and the absence of the lord from the castle should not
be taken as an indication that everything was quiet.
The Earl of Buchan's style of lordship certainly
contributed to the unrest, but it was the death
of his wife Euphemia, Countess of Ross,
which would cause the biggest upset.

Above: A warrior in the service of the
Lords of the Isles. In the late-medieval era,
the Islesmen raided wealthy castles of
the Great Glen from their power bases
in the islands off the west coast.

Left: Finlaggan, the chief seat of
the Lords of the Isles on Islay.

The MacDonald lordship of the Isles was eager to gain control of the earldom of Ross. They exercised a powerful influence over a great swathe of the western seaboard of Scotland, but Ross lay between their territory and the Stewart lands. Stewart control of this earldom meant that the Lords of the Isles were effectively hemmed in.

In the 1390s, Donald of Islay, Lord of the Isles staked a claim for Ross through his wife Mariota, Euphemia's daughter by her first marriage. But Euphemia's son, Alexander Leslie, the new earl of Ross, had strong Stewart ties through his marriage to Robert III's niece. Indeed, the two families were linked by a complex network of family ties and marriages.

In 1395 Alastair Carrach, Donald's brother, seized Urquhart Castle, which was strategically important to the control of the earldom. Whether this was a first strike in the battle for Ross or an opportunistic raid is not clear, but further attacks on Moray followed.

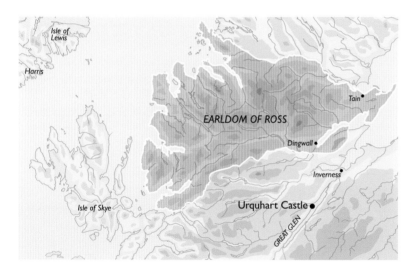

Above: A map showing the extent of the earldom of Ross in the 1390s. At this time, a power struggle broke out between the Stewart Earls of Buchan and the MacDonald Lords of the Isles for control of this territory.

Above: A birlinn carved on a gravestone on Iona. These small, nimble vessels were used by the Lords of the Isles to dominate the west coast of Scotland and to raid the Great Glen.

1384

ALEXANDER STEWART, EARL OF BUCHAN
known as the 'Wolf of Badenoch' acquires the castle. In 1390 he razes Elgin Cathedral.

1390s

DONALD OF ISLAY, LORD OF THE ISLES
stakes a claim to Ross. In 1395 his brother seizes Urquhart.

INSTABILITY AND UNREST

Further trouble came with the death of Alexander Leslie, Earl of Ross, in 1402. His heir, another Euphemia, was still a child.

Following her father's death, Euphemia, the young Countess of Ross, was taken to Edinburgh as the ward of her grandfather, Robert Stewart, Duke of Albany, who was then governor of Scotland.

Carrach saw his chance and launched an attack on Elgin, a vigorous show of force. Tensions over Ross culminated in the Battle of Harlaw, a bloody but inconclusive encounter, after which Donald, Lord of the Isles submitted to Robert Stewart.

Euphemia entered a nunnery in 1415, which rendered her legally dead. Donald's wife Mariota ceded her rights and Ross passed to the Stewarts. Urquhart was given to the earl of Mar in 1420, although the castle remained under the control of royal constables.

After James I's murder in 1437, Alexander MacDonald took the estate back but failed to retake the castle. Urquhart was then maintained by the constable, Thomas Oglivy, an able administrator but not the equal of the great military men of years past. Urquhart was managed as an outpost of Inverness Castle. It remained defensible, but the fact that it remained untaken despite being surrounded by the MacDonald-held estate suggests it was not as strategically important as it once was.

Exchequer accounts from the time show major expenditure on repair and new building at Urquhart and Inverness Castles, but we do not know how these funds were spent. Castle building in Scotland at this time emphasised the main tower house. Urquhart's many buildings – designed to accommodate the large retinues of the great lordships of the 1300s – were no longer needed.

Below: Loch Ness, the longest body of water in the Great Glen. In medieval times, it was quicker and easier to travel by water than by road.

Alexander died in 1449, and was succeeded as Lord of the Isles by his son, John. John married Elizabeth Livingston, daughter of the king's chamberlain, in an attempt to bond the royal court and the lordship, but the match failed and John rose against James II. He took the castles of Urquhart, Inverness and Ruthven, installing his father-in-law, James Livingston, as constable at Urquhart. Rather than crush this challenge to his authority, James chose to grant Urquhart Castle to Earl John for the duration of his life.

However, the earl's continued attempts to undermine the Crown in favour of the lordship eventually undermined his position. In 1476, after the king discovered he had agreed a secret treaty with King Edward IV of England, he was stripped of the earldom of Ross. The strategic estate of Urquhart was entrusted to George Gordon, 2nd Earl of Huntly, at that time the most powerful figure in north-east Scotland.

Top left: Four of the carved West Highland graveslabs found on Iona. They were created to mark the burial places of important Islesmen.

Top right: The graveslab of Gilbert de Greenlaw, who died fighting the Islesmen at the Battle of Harlaw in 1411.

Right: Arrowheads found at Urquhart, evidence of armed struggle at the site.

1411

ROBERT STEWART, DUKE OF ALBANY subdues the Lords of the Isles temporarily at the indecisive Battle of Harlaw. As a result he is able to reclaim Urquhart.

1462

EDWARD IV OF ENGLAND agrees a secret treaty with John, Earl of Ross and Lord of the Isles, granting him control of the Highlands in return for support of the English cause.

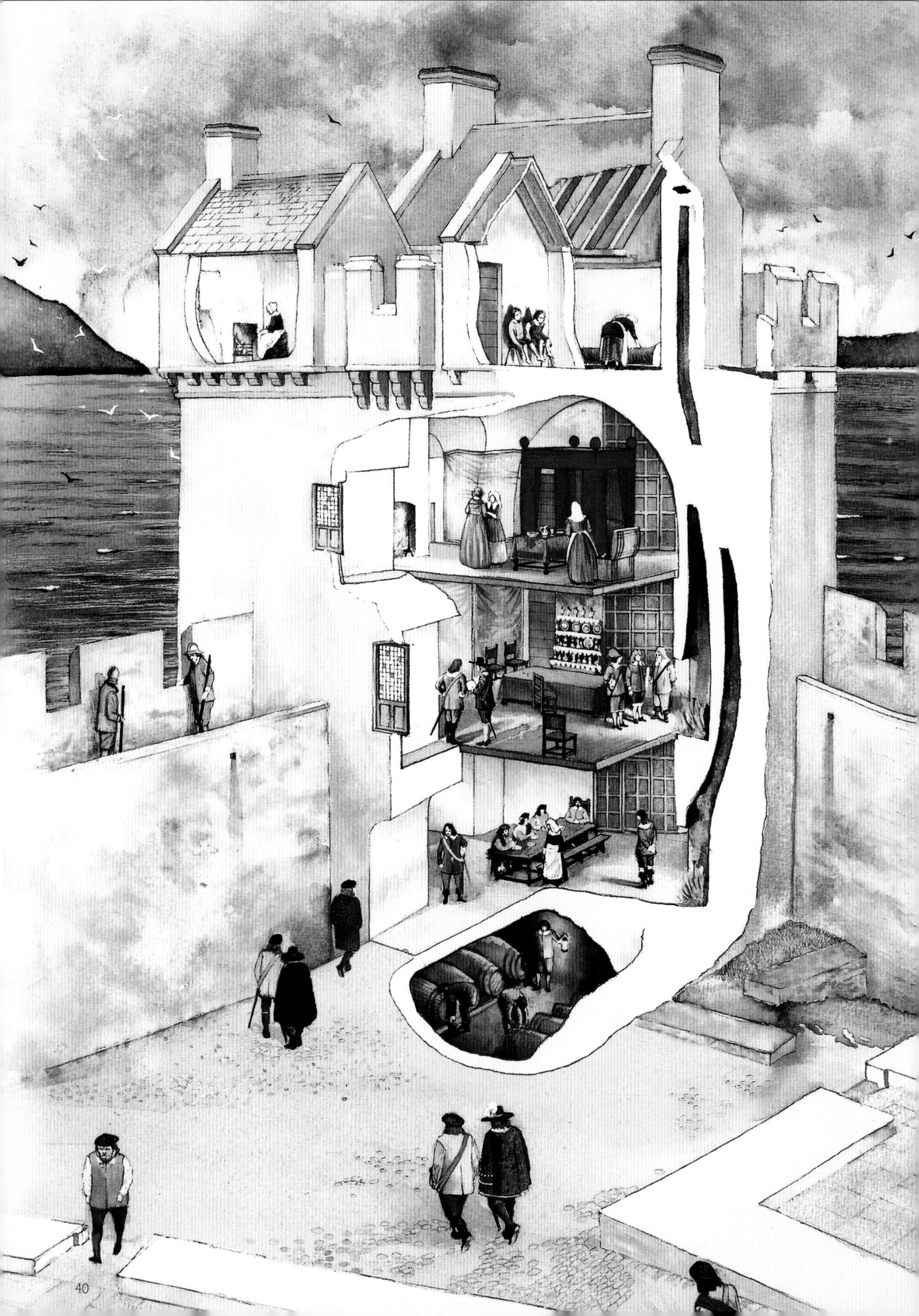

URQUHART AND THE CHIEFS OF GRANT

The Earl of Huntly administered Urquhart as a royal agent, but this did not bring stability to the glen, which had suffered considerable impoverishment during its years of unrest.

There is no mention of the castle in the Exchequer Rolls at this time, perhaps indicating that its position was also diminished. Continuing arguments with the MacLean allies of Clan Donald over ownership led to further devastation. Huntly sought arbitration, which found in favour of the Crown. Huntly then leased Urquhart to Sir Duncan Grant of Freuchie.

In 1485, Duncan left Urquhart to his grandson, John 'the Red Bard'. Eventually John brought something like order back to Urquhart. Although his main residence was Castle Grant, the Red Bard was closely involved in running the estate.

He was also the beneficiary of a quieter period in the castle's history. James IV acknowledged the Bard's achievement in 1509, granting the lordship to the Grant family. The estate was divided into three baronies, split between John and two of his sons, making it easier to administer and maintain.

John took the barony of Urquhart for himself. As well as paying duty to the king and providing military service, he was required to rehabilitate the castle and the estate (see page 22). This is perhaps an indication of the poor state of the castle buildings at the time, and certainly that they were not fit for a lord of the 1500s.

The Grants' remodelling of the castle is best represented by the Grant Tower, a five-storey tower house which stands at the north of the promontory, on the site formerly occupied by the donjon (see page 22). Although this can be dated to the 1500s, we cannot be sure exactly when it was built. It may well have been added after the raids which terrorised the glen well into that century.

← N

Opposite: The Grant Tower as it may have looked when in use, around the mid-1500s.

Left: The whole castle complex as it may have looked during the Grant era. By this time, the buildings around the summit were not in use and had fallen into disrepair.

1509

JAMES IV
charters the lordship of Urquhart to the Grant family, requiring them to build a stronghold and exert control in the region.

1513

THE BATTLE OF FLODDEN
wipes out James IV and many of his supporters, leaving the Great Glen again vulnerable to attack by the Islesmen.

THE MACDONALD RAIDS

The death of John MacDonald did not bring an end to the ambitions of the Islesmen. More uprisings followed, as others attempted to prove themselves worthy of the lordship.

The instability caused by James IV's death at Flodden in 1513 encouraged Donald MacDonald of Lochalsh to invade the glen, looting and killing and capturing the castle. John Grant's appeal for recompense survives, and records that they took:

'pottis, pannis, kettilie, nop [napkins], beddis, schetis, blancatis, coueringis, coddis [pillows], fische, flesche, breid, aill, cheis, butter and vyther stuf of houshald, and salt hydis, extending be gude estimatioun to the soume of ane hundredth pund with the mair.'

They also took 740 bolls (161kl) of bere barley, 1,040 bolls (227kl) of oats, 300 cattle and 1,000 sheep.

The Red Bard responded by turning not to violence, but to politics. He married his daughter to Donald Cameron and so allied himself to a powerful local family who, he hoped, could aid him against the MacDonalds. John was succeeded in 1528 by his son James, known to history as 'James of the Raids'.

James's intervention in a succession dispute within Clanranald led to raids in 1543 and in 1545, when the MacDonald clans of Clanranald, Glengarry, Keppoch and MacIain 'swept the land of every hoof and article of food or furniture which they could find'.

This is the best documented of all Highland raids, and a staggering amount was taken. However, the Great Raid proved to be the last the inhabitants of Urquhart saw of the men from the west. Gradually the tenor of pastoral life was resumed in the glen, and the Grants began to repair the battered castle. Work was apparently still going on into the following century.

Above: The Great Raid of 1545, when the MacDonalds stripped the castle and its estate of a vast haul of goods and livestock.

DAYLIGHT ROBBERY:
THE SPOILS OF 1545

Despite earlier raids, Urquhart was clearly very wealthy at the time of the Great Raid. The raiders must have been delighted with the enormous haul of booty from the castle and its estates, which included:

3 great boats
3,377 sheep
2,355 cattle
2,204 goats
395 horses
122 swine
64 geese
3,206 bolls (700kl) of oats
1,427 bolls (311kl) of bere barley
60 ells (56m) of cloth
12 feather beds with bolsters, blankets
   and sheets tables and other items of furniture,
   to a total value of £323
a chest containing £300
20 artillery pieces, with gunpowder
stands of armour
doors, locks and yetts (iron gates)
2 brewing vats
6 roasting spits
5 pots and 6 pans

Right: A Highland cow of the kind that would have been reared at Urquhart in the 1500s. Today, they have been bred with orange coats, but at this time most would have been black, and smaller than modern cattle. Other kinds of livestock, such as sheep and horses, would have looked quite different from most of the breeds that now inhabit Scottish farmlands.

1528

1545

HECTOR BOECE
laments the 'rewinous wallis' of Urquhart Castle in the aftermath of renewed raids by the Islesmen.

MACDONALD RAIDERS
carry off every vestige of portable wealth from the castle and its estate, though this marks an end to their forays up the glen.

DECLINE AND FALL

Urquhart was never the primary residence of the Grants, and its infrequent occupancy probably led to neglect. The castle's last occupant was Marie Ogilvy, mother of James Grant, 7th Laird of Freuchie.

In 1637, the 6th Laird of Freuchie died and was succeeded by his 21-year-old son, James Grant. The following year, the new laird became a signatory to the National Covenant, a document drawn up in Edinburgh to resist Charles I's attempt to introduce a form of Anglican worship to the Scottish church. This led ultimately to civil war between the Covenanters and forces loyal to the king.

The 6th Laird's widow, Marie Ogilvy, had secured the right to reside in the castle after her husband's death. She proved an unpopular landlord, whose heavy-handed approach to imposing order on the estate led to local resentment.

The situation came to a head at Christmas 1644, when Urquhart Castle was attacked by Covenanters from Inverness, with assistance from the dowager's disgruntled tenants. The previous year, the 7th Laird had refused to endorse the Solemn League and Covenant, a new document calling for the establishment of Presbyterian worship across Britain. The castle was ransacked and everything movable carried off. Marie Ogilvy was run out of the glen and never returned.

In 1647, the laird commissioned an inventory of the castle's sadly depleted contents: a few beds, tables, benches, chairs and an old chest. As for the rest of the once-mighty castle, it was 'without any kynd of uther wairis, pleneishing, goodis or geir whatsumever … except allenarlie [only] bare walls'. The total value was reckoned at £20.

Top left: James Grant, 7th Laird of Freuchie, who inherited Urquhart in 1637. The castle's last occupant was his mother, Marie Ogilvy.

Left: His wife, Lady Mary Stewart.

Following Oliver Cromwell's invasion of Scotland in 1650, new forts were built at either end of the Great Glen; Inverlochy (now Fort William) and Inverness. But the English chose not to garrison Urquhart, content to leave the patrolling of Loch Ness to a ship, called by one observer 'a statly friggot'.

Urquhart Castle was garrisoned for the last time during the troubles that followed the exile of the Catholic King James VII, and his replacement by the Protestant joint monarchs William II and Mary II. In November 1689 the castle was garrisoned by three companies of Highlanders from Lord Strathnaver's and Grant's Regiment of Foot, under the command of Captain Grant. They were besieged by Jacobite supporters of the deposed king under MacDonell of Glengarry.

'I am certainly inform'd that 500 of the rebells were come to Urquett,' wrote Sir James Leslie to Lord Melville, commander of King William's Scottish army, in December 1689. 'They threatned the castle, but I looke upon it to be in little dainger, they [the garrison] haveing a fortnight's or three weeks's provisions.'

Glengarry eventually had to retreat to defend his own lands, but the garrison remained at the castle for another two years. When they left the castle, they reportedly blew up some of the buildings to stop the enemy from holding it again. The results of their action are still visible in the great chunks of masonry lying beside the gatehouse. The damage was never repaired.

Above: The Protestant King William II (left) and his wife Queen Mary II (centre), who reigned jointly following the exile of the Catholic King James VII (right) in December 1688.

1637

MARIE OGILVY
newly widowed mother of the 7th Laird, moves into the castle, becoming its last high-status resident. In 1644, she is robbed and driven out by Covenanters.

1689-92

GOVERNMENT FORCES
garrison Urquhart Castle for more than two years. On leaving in January 1692, they destroy the gatehouse with gunpowder.

A NOBLE RUIN

Bereft of residents and soldiers, Urquhart soon declined. But as attitudes changed, the ancient castle came to be viewed as a noble ruin in a majestic setting.

When the last garrison marched out in 1692, the castle buildings rapidly fell into decay. People from the glen came and salvaged what they could for use elsewhere – the best of the stonework, the lead from the roofs, the timber, the ironwork and so on. On 19 February 1715, part of the Grant Tower came crashing to the ground during a violent storm, leaving a gaping hole in one side of the building.

A survey of the castle and grounds made about 1770 shows the ancient castle buildings roofless, but someone was living in a long, narrow building immediately beyond the castle ditch, close to where the large kiln remains today. The building lay at the corner of a large garden.

Encouraged by the writings of Sir Walter Scott and others, people began to take a greater interest in ruined castles, beyond their value as salvage yards. Set against one of the most dramatic of Highland landscapes, Urquhart Castle drew an increasing number of visitors, to gaze in awe, to think on times past, to sketch and to paint.

Left: Urquhart Castle romantically depicted on the title page of *The Tourist's Ramble in the Highlands*, a collection of prints by the French landscape artist Michel Bouquet, published in 1850.

Above: An engraving of the castle by Louis Haghe, based on a sketch by J.G. Hamilton, dating from the mid-1800s. As was common in antiquarian illustrations of this period, the architectural details are not entirely accurate.

They included the Scottish poet Robert Burns, the English poet Samuel Taylor Coleridge, who viewed the castle from the far side of the loch, and the English artist John Everett Millais, who visited Scotland following the death of his son and produced a haunting painting of the castle (see pages 24–5).

In 1884, Caroline, Countess Dowager of Seafield, widow of the 7th Earl of Grant, assumed control of her son's estates, including Urquhart and Glenmoriston. When she died, in 1911, her will instructed that Urquhart's frail ruins be entrusted

into State care. On 6 October 1913, a guardianship agreement was signed, transferring responsibility for the castle's upkeep to the Commissioners of His Majesty's Works and Public Buildings.

Historic Scotland, as successor to that body, continues to maintain the ancient ruins to this day.

Above left: The English poet Samuel Taylor Coleridge, who was among the visitors to be inspired by Urquhart.

Top right: The English artist John Everett Millais, who spent several months in Drumnadrochit, where he painted Urquhart Castle as *The Tower of Strength* (1878).

1715

THE GRANT TOWER
is partially destroyed by a violent February storm.

1884

CAROLINE, COUNTESS DOWAGER OF SEAFIELD
takes ownership of Urquhart Castle. When she dies in 1911, she entrusts the castle into State care.

Urquhart Castle is one of more than 50 Historic Scotland properties in the Highlands. A selection of others is shown below.

FORT GEORGE

Built in 1746–69, in the aftermath of the last Jacobite Rising, Fort George was a state-of-the-art military installation and is still in use by the army.

- 6 miles west of Nairn off the A96
- Open all year
- 01667 460232
- Approx **21 miles** from Urquhart Castle

DALLAS DHU DISTILLERY

In use from 1899 until 1983, this historic distillery has been preserved intact, allowing visitors to discover the whisky production process.

- 2 miles south of Forres off the A940
- Open all year. Winter closed Thu and Fri
- 01309 676548
- Approx **45 miles** from Urquhart Castle

ELGIN CATHEDRAL

A marvel of medieval church architecture, largely ruined but still wonderfully impressive, with a fascinating collection of carved masonry details.

- In Elgin on the A96
- Open all year. Winter closed Thu and Fri
- 01343 547171
- Approx **55 miles** from Urquhart Castle

SPYNIE PALACE

The medieval residence of the bishops of Moray, now dominated by David's Tower, a grand six-storey residence begun around 1470 for Bishop David Stewart.

- 2 miles N of Elgin off the A941
- Open all year. Winter weekends only
- 01343 546358
- Approx **57 miles** from Urquhart Castle

For more information on all Historic Scotland sites, visit www.historic-scotland.gov.uk
To order tickets and a wide range of gifts, visit www.historic-scotland.gov.uk/shop

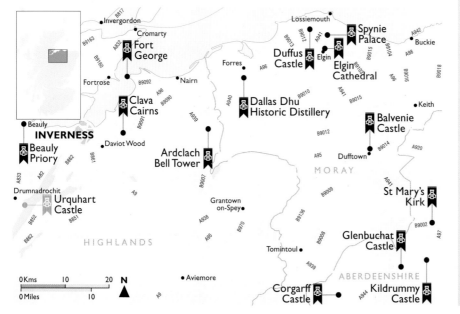

Key to facilities

Car parking	P
Bus/coach parking	
Bicycle parking	
Closed for lunch	
Toilets	
Interpretive display	
Reasonable wheelchair access	
Accessible toilets	
Visitor centre	
Restaurant/cafe	
Shop	
Picnic area	
Childrens quiz available	
Tea/coffee making facilities	
No dogs	